GEOMETRY

Penny Dowdy

Crabtree Publishing Company
www.crabtreebooks.com

Author: Penny Dowdy
Coordinating editor: Chester Fisher
Series editor: Jessica Cohn
Editors: Reagan Miller, Molly Aloian
Proofreader: Crystal Sikkens
Project coordinator: Robert Walker
Production coordinator: Margaret Amy Salter
Prepress technician: Margaret Amy Salter
Logo design: Samantha Crabtree
Design: Tarang Saggar (Q2AMEDIA)
Cover design: Harleen Mehta (Q2AMEDIA)
Project manager: Santosh Vasudevan (Q2AMEDIA)
Art direction: Rahul Dhiman (Q2AMEDIA)
Photo research: Anju Pathak (Q2AMEDIA)

Photographs:
Fotolia: Snezana Skundric: p. 19
Istockphoto: Phil Date: p. 7; Stefanie Timmermann: p. 5
Jupiter Images: PhotoAlto, Odilon Dimier: p. 11; Image Source: p. 15
Shutterstock: Robert J. Beyers II: p. 9; Cabania: cover (girl);
    DanieleDM: p. 17; Oleg Kozlov, Sophy Kozlova: p. 13;
    Johnny Lye: cover (blocks); Photo Create: p. 1;
    Vladislav Susoy: cover (black board); Donald R. Swartz: p. 21

Library and Archives Canada Cataloguing in Publication

Dowdy, Penny
    Geometry / Penny Dowdy.

(My path to math)
Includes index.
ISBN 978-0-7787-4340-8 (bound).--ISBN 978-0-7787-4358-3 (pbk.)

    1. Geometry--Juvenile literature. I. Title. II. Series: Dowdy, Penny.
My path to math.

QA445.5.D69 2008   j516   C2008-903484-8

Library of Congress Cataloging-in-Publication Data

Dowdy, Penny.
    Geometry / Penny Dowdy.
        p. cm. -- (My path to math)
    Includes index.
    ISBN-13: 978-0-7787-4358-3 (pbk. : alk. paper)
    ISBN-10: 0-7787-4358-6 (pbk. : alk. paper)
    ISBN-13: 978-0-7787-4340-8 (reinforced library binding : alk. paper)
    ISBN-10: 0-7787-4340-3 (reinforced library binding : alk. paper)
    1. Geometry--Juvenile literature. I. Title. II. Series.

    QA445.5.D69 2009
    516--dc22
                                2008023534

Crabtree Publishing Company

www.crabtreebooks.com   1-800-387-7650

Published in Canada
Crabtree Publishing
616 Welland Ave.
St. Catharines, Ontario
L2M 5V6

Published in the United States
Crabtree Publishing
PMB16A
350 Fifth Ave., Suite 3308
New York, NY 10118

Published in the United Kingdom
Crabtree Publishing
White Cross Mills
High Town, Lancaster
LA1 4XS

Published in Australia
Crabtree Publishing
386 Mt. Alexander Rd.
Ascot Vale (Melbourne)
VIC 3032

Contents

Lines

Shapes and lines are everywhere you look. There are different kinds of lines. One kind of line is a **straight line**. A straight line does not curve. You can see many straight lines on steps.

A **curved line** is not straight. A curved line can bend. It can twist. It can turn.

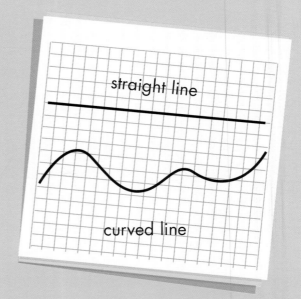

straight line

curved line

Activity Box

Imagine if your bedroom had curved walls. Draw what it would look like.

The top of each step
is a straight line.

Circles

Flat shapes you see are **plane shapes**. Shapes on paper are plane shapes. The faces of things, like pizza, can be plane shapes, too.

A **circle** is one kind of plane shape. A circle has no **corners**. It has no straight lines. A circle is a flat shape made from a curved line.

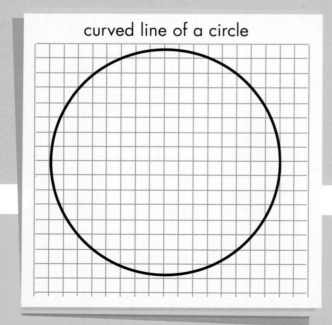

curved line of a circle

Pizza comes in the shape of a circle!

Triangles

A **triangle** is another plane shape. A triangle has three straight sides. It has three corners.

Look at the sign at the top of the picture on the next page. Its three sides are the same size. The sides of triangles are not always the same size, though. Triangles can have sides of different sizes.

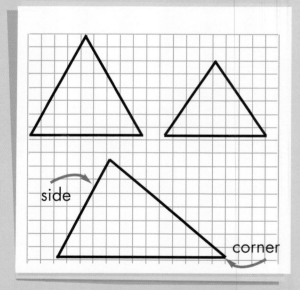

side

corner

Activity Box

Corners are spots where two lines meet. Which triangle above has the widest corner of all the corners shown?

YIELD

TO ONCOMING TRAFFIC

What is the shape of the top sign?

9

Four Sides

Squares and **rectangles** are plane shapes. They both have four straight sides. They both have four corners.

A square has four straight sides that are the same size. In a rectangle, the **opposite** sides are the same size. Opposite means across from or facing.

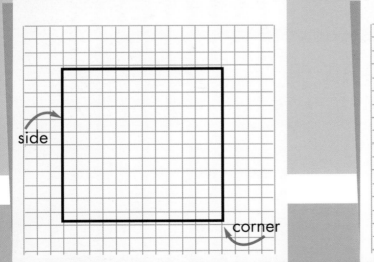

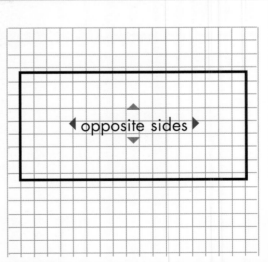

Count the squares. They are numbered for you!

Spheres

A **solid shape** is not flat like a plane shape. You can wrap your hands around a solid shape.

A **sphere** is one kind of solid shape. A sphere is shaped like a ball. When you play with a ball, you play with a sphere.

flat drawing of a sphere

A sphere is round.

Cones

A **cone** is a solid shape. Have you ever seen an orange cone on the road?

One end of a cone is a circle. The other end comes to a point. If you set a cone on the circle, it stands. If you set it on the point, it tips over!

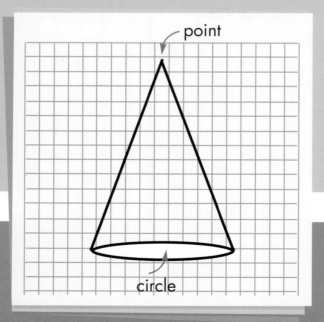

point

circle

How many cones do you count?

Pyramids

A **pyramid** is a solid shape with triangles on its sides. The sides meet in a point at one end.

A pyramid is like a cone, but not in every way. Pyramids have triangles on their sides. On the end across from the point is a shape with straight sides.

side

end with straight sides

point

Activity Box

How are pyramids and cones the same? How are they different?

Buildings have many shapes.

Prisms

Prisms are solid shapes with three or more sides. The sides of prisms are like rectangles.

The ends of a prism are shapes with straight edges. The ends can look like triangles or many other shapes. A prism can stand on a side or an end.

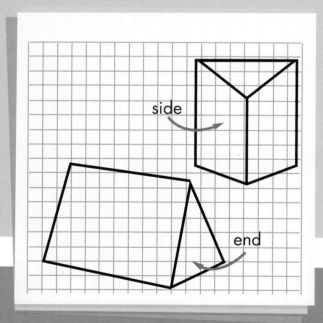

side

end

Activity Box

Where are the prisms in your home and school?

A tall building is a kind of prism.

Cubes

Cubes are special prisms. Cubes are prisms with six sides. All six sides are squares.

What happens when you turn a square on its side? It looks the same! What happens when you turn a cube on its side? It looks the same, too.

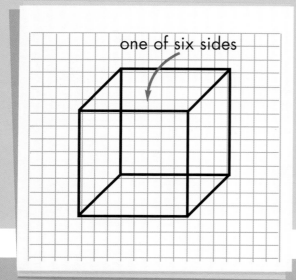

one of six sides

Activity Box

Is a shoebox a cube? Why or why not?

Someone made art from a big, red cube.

Glossary

circle A plane shape made of one curved edge

cone A solid shape with a circle on one end and a point at the other

corner The place where two lines meet

cube A prism with squares on all sides and ends

curved line A line with a beginning, an end, and bends in between

opposite Across from or facing

plane shape A shape that is flat

prism A solid shape with rectangles on three or more sides and ends with straight edges

pyramid A solid shape with straight sides on one end and a point on the other

rectangle A plane shape with four sides and four corners

solid shape A shape that a person could wrap his or her hands around

sphere A solid round shape

square A plane shape with four sides of the same size and four corners that look the same

straight line A line with a beginning, an end, and no curve

triangle A plane shape with three sides and three corners

Index

Printed in the U.S.A. — CG